Finding the Missing
PEACE
to Life's Puzzle

Ethel E. Reeves, MEd

WESTBOW
PRESS®
A DIVISION OF THOMAS NELSON
& ZONDERVAN

WestBow Press books may be ordered through booksellers or by contacting:

WestBow Press
A Division of Thomas Nelson & Zondervan
1663 Liberty Drive
Bloomington, IN 47403
www.westbowpress.com
844-714-3454

ISBN: 978-1-6642-3621-9 (sc)
ISBN: 978-1-6642-3622-6 (hc)
ISBN: 978-1-6642-3620-2 (e)

Library of Congress Control Number: 2021911178

Print information available on the last page.

WestBow Press rev. date: 7/16/2021

This book is dedicated to my two amazing children, Dakota and Jacquelle, who stood by me in my pursuit of peace. On days when I felt I could not go on, they were the wind beneath my wings both individually and collectively.

In memory of my parents, James H. "Slick" Reeves Jr., and Jacqueline Paige Reeves. You both instilled the values in me that I operate in daily. Thank you for showing me the way. On days when I miss you the most, I reflect on the lessons you taught me.

Kelvin, my one and only brother, thank you for modeling what "don't worry about it" looks like.

To my iron sharpeners, who are too numerous to name, thank you!

Most importantly, I thank God for who He is. I am grateful for what He has done, what He is doing, and what He will do.

INTRODUCTION

As a child, I always liked to solve things. I remember sitting for hours, solving logic problems, and getting really excited when I figured out which girl was first in line, standing beside the girl who had on the pink dress with the polka dot bow, who was the older sister to the boy with red hair, who stood at the end of the line in a striped shirt. If all that is confusing to you, just remember that I said I absolutely loved getting to the end of that puzzle.

With maturity, I found that life was not as simple as figuring out a cute little logic puzzle. Instead, I found that there were people and situations that I just did not understand. Circumstances occurred that were completely out of control and completely out of *my* control, yet every day, life continued. And because I have to be totally honest, choices I made sometimes caused situations to occur, thus creating more life experiences. To get through these experiences, I had to place one foot in front of the other as I went from day to day.

The pieces to life's puzzle, whether it's a logic puzzle, a jigsaw puzzle, or any other puzzle, can come at you in all forms and in any shape or size, at any time. Sometimes multiple pieces to your puzzle come at the same time. Anyone who enjoys doing puzzles knows that you must find the corners first. In life, when the corners cannot be found and the image of the finished product has faded, it may seem as though the puzzle is not worth completing. If you're living with a spouse who decides they no longer want to be married, or maybe your children make poor decisions in life—such as their grades dropping, or maybe they're experimenting with drugs, alcohol, or sex—it may seem that life is not worth living because you can't see how things are going to work out for you.

Stress is another piece of the puzzle. Did I mention that a piece sometimes comes in the form of your stress level being so high that you're experiencing brain fog that is not evident to anyone but you? Or maybe your supervisor is on the warpath and you are in the direct line of fire. If you've ever been searching frantically for your cell phone only to find that you are talking on it, that's stress. Or maybe you're looking for your glasses and find that they are on your face. It's all part of life's puzzle. Finding the missing "peace" allows me to smile now, but at the time, none of these pieces gave me anything to smile about.

With so much happening, how does one truly find the missing *peace* to life's puzzle? I am so glad you asked. Keep reading, and I will share with you some of the things that helped me as I sought to find the missing peace to life's puzzle. Please understand that although my story and the puzzles that I have had to put together will not necessarily be like yours, all of us are created in the image and likeness of Christ, and that in itself is a beautiful image to behold. Along with that, we are admonished to pursue peace. "Run from anything that stimulates youthful lusts. Instead, pursue righteous living, faithfulness, love, and *peace*. Enjoy the companionship of those who call on the Lord with pure hearts" (2 Timothy 2:22 NLT, emphasis added).

From experience, I can tell you that life is worth living and that finding the missing peace in life is not only critical to success, but it is necessary.

As long as you have breath in your body and blood running warm through your veins, you have an opportunity to manifest your place of peace. Pause and read Lamentations 3:22–23. What are these scriptures saying to you?

_____

_____

_____

_____

_____

_____

_____

_____

_____

_____

_____

_____

_____

_____

_____

_____

_____

_____

_____

_____

Your current situation is not your final destination.

Each new day is a day of opportunity.

REFLECTION

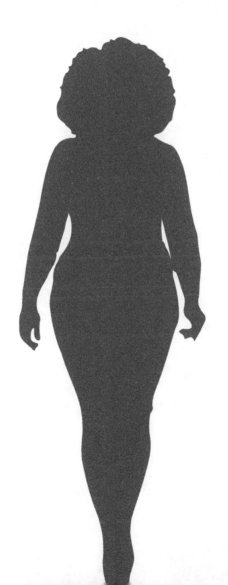

Do you have an image of what your life should be like? Describe what that image looks like.

_____

_____

_____

_____

_____

_____

_____

_____

_____

_____

_____

_____

_____

_____

_____

_____

_____

_____

Have you ever thought about what life would be like in its most peaceful state?

_____

_____

_____

_____

_____

_____

_____

_____

_____

_____

_____

_____

_____

_____

_____

_____

_____

_____

_____

When you think of peace, what is the first thing that comes to mind? Explain.

_____

_____

_____

_____

_____

_____

_____

_____

_____

_____

_____

_____

_____

_____

_____

_____

_____

_____

_____

PEACE

What is peace anyway? Why would one want to "find" it?

What a great question! Before I define *peace* and share information about its importance, I have a question. What is the alternative to having peace in life?

It may be easier to answer this question than to find a definition for *peace*. Without it, there is both internal and external turmoil. Our mental wellness may be under attack. Thoughts can be negative, incomplete, or simply nonexistent. They may be there one minute and gone the next. Without peace, those negative thoughts lead to unkind words or deeds that could land you in hot water, making you regret that you even allowed those thoughts to enter your mind, much less control your actions. Without peace, one wanders through life both helpless and hopeless.

But wait a minute—there are people in life who thrive on chaos and drama. Some people pursue drama and seem to enjoy it—emphasis on the word *seem*. Their lives are filled with pieces that, in many cases, do not belong to their puzzles. Have you ever tried to put together a puzzle only to find that the pieces did not even belong to that puzzle? What do you do? Usually one of two things: you either spend time making sure all the puzzle pieces are in the right boxes so you can then work on them, or you simply throw away the whole puzzle. Nonetheless, living a life of drama and turmoil is a waste of time.

So again, I ask, what is peace? Why would one want to find peace?

Merriam-Webster defines *peace* as:

1: a state of tranquility or quiet: such as
   a) freedom civil disturbance;
   b) a state of security or order within a community provided for by law or custom;
2: freedom from disquieting or oppressive thoughts or emotions
3: harmony in personal relations
   4a: a state or period of mutual concord between governments;
   4b: a pact or agreement to end hostilities between those who have been at war or in a state of enmity.

I like to think of peace as that state where I am free from disturbance and content with the situation(s) at hand. As a believer, I understand that peace is something that belongs to me. "God is not the author of confusion but of peace" (1 Corinthians 14:33 KJV). Although this speaks to behavior in the churches, I understand that, as a believer, I am the church, and this applies to me in all situations. God is the author of peace.

I am also reminded that I am meant to pursue peace. Psalm 34:14 (AMPC) states, "Depart from evil and do good; seek, inquire for, and crave peace and pursue [go after] it!" This means I need to make some choices and decisions in life. When I recognize that I am in a confused state, I must assess the situation and then move quickly in the direction of peace. Sometimes, this means saying no. By the way, *no* is a complete sentence. It does not require further explanations or excuses—just a *no*. On many occasions, I say no with a smile, but even the smile is more of a courtesy than a requirement. On days when I feel like I am crashing mentally, I am reminded of Isaiah 26:3, which tells me that God will keep me in perfect peace as I keep my mind stayed on Him. Peace belongs to me, and it belongs to you, too, but it is something that we must go after. Hebrew 12:14 (NKJV) admonishes us to "pursue peace with all people, and holiness, without which no one will see the Lord." Let me pause right here. Holding on to bitterness and anger is neither helpful nor healthy. I heard someone say that walking in unforgiveness is like drinking poison and expecting someone else to die. You are not at peace if anyone is occupying your mental space. *What do you mean, Ethel?* If you pause just for a minute, consider the things that you are thinking about. If those things lead to anger and resentment, then something is wrong. When you think of a particular person and evil thoughts surface—or worse, if you are talking about that person and speaking evil things about that individual, you are walking in unforgiveness. Let it go! Those who have harmed you or who you are allowing to rent space in your head are not even thinking about you. They hurt you, but they may not have known they hurt you and have moved on. They are living their best lives. They are not thinking about you! Let them go! Release them *now*, in Jesus's name.

You may say, "No, Ethel, you don't understand. They deliberately hurt me, and they are talking about me and … and … and …"

Okay! I may not understand, but I do understand this: "Vengeance is mine, I will repay, saith the Lord" (Romans 12:19 KJV). In the same verse, God tells us not to avenge ourselves. We must leave things in God's hands and let Him deal with those who hurt His children. Let it go! Is it easy? If I'm honest with you, and I am, then no, indeed, it's not easy—at first. As you gain more understanding and allow yourself to grow and develop, it will become easier. God is not a liar. He will take care of His own. You may never see or hear about how God handles your haters, but trust His Word. He will take care of His own.

You will experience trials and conflict in life. Things will not always be easy. "Many are the afflictions of the righteous: but the Lord delivers him out of them all" (Psalms 34:19 NKJV). We will go through things in life, but we must know that we are doing just that—going through. We cannot stop living when trouble rears its head. We must keep going and keep living. If we do not quit, we will get through it. There is nothing that we encounter in this life that takes God by surprise. He wants us to talk with Him. Proverbs 3:5–6 (NKJV) says it best: "Trust in the Lord with all your heart, and lean not on your own understanding; In all your ways acknowledge Him, And He shall direct your paths."

Understand that as you are going through, there may be opportunities to *grow* through. Begin asking, "Lord, what would you have me learn while I'm in this situation?" Ask yourself, "What can I learn about myself while going through this situation?" You will find that if you look at the situation as a growth opportunity, good will come out of it.

Peace.

When something is at peace, it is resting. It is not moving or troubled.

Peace.

We must become comfortable being in a peaceful state. We do not have to "go" all the time.

Peace.

It begins with us. We are responsible for maintaining our peace.

So, how does one pursue peace in a world filled with chaos and when all the pieces to life's puzzle are in disarray? Let's talk about this pursuit.

THE PURSUIT

The pursuit of peace is an ongoing process. In every situation one encounters, you must decide to pursue peace. Have you ever been late getting up for work or school? What was your first response? I am sure there are many. There was a time in my home when this situation would elicit some colorful language, a little blaming, and then the throwing on of clothes and the search for the keys. Then, once I arrived at work, I would realize that there were no parking spaces close to the building, necessitating a fast walk into the building only to find that the meeting had already started, and the only empty seats were in the front of the room. Did I mention that my body would be glistening with perspiration and my laptop that I needed for the meeting was still in the car?

Is there a need to pursue peace in this situation? By all means. At that moment, choices must be made. Deep breaths always help, and so does smiling. I dare you to try it. Many times, our minds remain in overdrive, and before we know it our emotions take over. Anger or embarrassment causes us to react in a manner that would not occur in a more peaceful state. Maybe this specific situation is not one to which you can relate, and that's okay—but I am sure there has been a time when you wished you could just hit the proverbial reset button and start all over again. And that, my friend, is the answer. When life is coming at you fast and the pressure is on, make the decision to pursue peace in that instant. Hit your mental reset button. Own where you are and breathe.

A pursuit is a chase. I am blessed to have an energetic three-year-old grandson. He loves the outdoors and will take off running as soon as the door opens. Nana—a.k.a. me—then has to pursue him. The pursuit is never a straight journey to a specific destination. It usually takes me down the stairs, counterclockwise around the car, and then back in the other direction. Just when I think I have caught him, he will take off in another direction up the hill. This is the pursuit. I get tired because my energy level and physical abilities are not like those of a three-year-old. I begin to call his name and beg for him to stop running. He often looks at me, stops for a millisecond, and then takes off again. Because my grandson and his safety are important to me, I continue to pursue him despite my feelings, the pain in my knees, and the shortness of my breath. He matters, and so does my pursuit of him. On the other hand, if the ball that he loves to play with begins to roll down the hill, there will be no pursuit. Why not? Well, running at this point in my life is not my strength. The value of the ball is far less than the potential injuries that I could face chasing after it and, quite frankly, the ball can be replaced. It does not require a research study to quickly assess the situation and decide that the pursuit is just not worth it.

In life, there will be things, situations, and relationships that are worth the pursuit. There will also be things, situations, and relationships that are just not worth the time, energy, and effort to pursue them. Those things are not pieces to your life's puzzle. It doesn't matter how you turn them; they will not fit into your puzzle.

The pursuit must be in line with your purpose. Why would one pursue anything that does not add value to life? Consider your "why" and your worth. Will what you have to go through in your pursuit be worth it in the end? It may very well be a necessary pursuit. Pause, reflect, and count the costs associated with including this piece in your puzzle. No one likes to get to the end of a puzzle only to discover they have the wrong piece or a missing piece left. Determine what is needed in order to stay in the pursuit. Will it be worth it once you have it?

I have always stated that the only way I would get my doctorate degree is if someone else pays for it. Some of my friends and colleagues completed doctoral programs, and I cheered them on from the sidelines. They would encourage me to start my own program, and I would state, "The only way I will get my doctorate is if someone else pays for it." (As a side note, your words have creative ability, but that's another book.)

As my mother's health began to decline, out of nowhere came an opportunity to get my doctorate ... tuition-free. Again, watch what you say. As a caregiver for my mother, I had to decide if this was a piece to life's puzzle or a mere distraction. I had to count the cost. Would putting in the work now be worth it in three years? I prayed and asked God for direction, and I trust that in another two years, I'll sign my name as Dr. Ethel E. Reeves. The pursuit has been worth it. You see, I blocked out all the thoughts about what other people were doing and began to focus on the blessing that I had in being able to take care of my mother. And, although it was difficult, it was necessary. So while she was resting, I was reading. It gave me time to be with her and also to take the steps toward one of my goals. Please hear me when I say that it was not easy by any stretch of the imagination, but it was necessary. My mother transitioned before I could finish this book, and she will not be here to see me receive my doctoral degree. But the peace I have and continue to carry in my heart, knowing that I did my best for her while she lived, was all worth the pursuit.

Second, people will be an important part of your pursuit. This may not be easy to swallow, but learn quickly that not everyone will be there for you. There will be those who are with you now who cannot be a part of the journey as you pursue peace. You have been tolerating them, and you love them. You want to help them. You believe in them. I know all about it. But in this season, you must make the decision to release people who are not a productive part of your pursuit. Brace yourself. Are you ready?

Some of the people that you release will be family members. Breathe. Now, when I say to release them, this is what I mean. I want you to love them with the love of Jesus. However, do not allow any negativity or weight that they bring cause you to delay or stop your pursuit of peace.

There will be people who appear to celebrate you on your journey who, in reality, are only staying close to you to find out what you are doing. Please be aware. Love them, but also guard your heart, your time, and your plans.

Haters—yes, accept now that you will have haters. When people you do not know say negative or derogatory things to or about you, it typically does not matter. Again, you do not know them, and they don't really know you. Prepare yourself for the hurt that comes from those who have been close to you. When it happens, do not allow the hurt to paralyze you to the point that your pursuit comes to a screeching halt.

Recognize that we are human. Jealousy is pervasive, and unfortunately, when people feel threatened or inferior, they respond differently. Hurting people will hurt other people. Healed people will be a part of the healing of others. If your circle of friends gets smaller in your pursuit of peace, continue the pursuit. Remember your "why," and recognize that not everyone will be able to go on the journey with you. Recognize, too, that your haters really should be your motivators. They are going to talk whether you're doing good or bad, so just keep doing life on your level. The best advice given to me was from one of my mentors, who shared that I should go so far in life that I can't hear my haters.

As you remember your "why," also remember the promises that God has given to each of us. According to 2 Corinthians 1:20 (NKJV), "For all the promises of God in Him are yes, and in Him amen, to the glory of God through us." God wants us to receive His best. He gets the glory in our victory. He delights Himself in our prosperity. He is Abba Father! He is the one who created us in His image and His likeness.

As His children, we have the authority to use His name. God is faithful. He is willing, and He is able. I love reading Ephesians 3:20–21 (NKJV). It states, "Now to Him who is able to do exceedingly abundantly above all that we ask or think, according to the power that works in us, to Him be glory in the church by Christ Jesus to all generations, forever and ever. Amen."

These verses cause me to think bigger. Because God can do exceedingly more than we can, what are we thinking? Why not think God-sized thoughts? God is able. We have the power in us, according to His Word, to call on God. Your pursuit is what you say it is. If your pursuit of peace looks like an impossibility, then involve God. See yourself where you want to be and begin moving in that direction. God is with us. Once you get ahold of who you are and whose you are, there is no stopping you.

REFLECTION

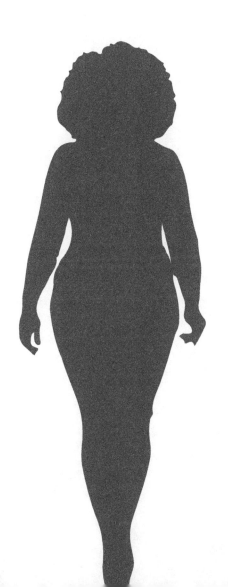

Will your pursuit bring you to that place that you have imagined?
Will the pursuit be worth it?

_____

_____

_____

_____

_____

_____

_____

_____

_____

_____

_____

_____

_____

_____

_____

_____

_____

_____

In your pursuit, are there things that you will need to say no to?

_____

_____

_____

_____

_____

_____

_____

_____

_____

_____

_____

_____

_____

_____

_____

_____

What God-sized thoughts are you having as you pursue peace?

_____

_____

_____

_____

_____

_____

_____

_____

_____

_____

_____

_____

_____

_____

_____

_____

_____

_____

Continue writing your God-sized thoughts. Are you thinking big enough?

_____

_____

_____

_____

_____

_____

_____

_____

_____

_____

_____

_____

_____

_____

_____

_____

_____

_____

_____

_____

Time management is important. And although it is important to live a balanced life, it is more important to live a life that is in alignment with God's Word and plans for our lives. Are all the things you're balancing a part of the plan? If not, rid yourself of those things and balance the rest in alignment with your goals and with God's plan for you. Examine what you are doing. You will find that there are things you can release so that you can make room for what truly matters.

Balance those things that are aligned with God's plan.

ENVIRONMENT

In order to remain unstoppable, look around you. Is there anything in your way that will cause distractions or obstacles? Address those. If you are always late to work, determine why. Is it because you do laundry and leave all your clothes folded in the baskets, which then forces you to go "in search of" every morning? Maybe you are burdened down with low or poor credit because you keep paying your bills late. Where do you keep your bills? Do you have a management system that will help remind you of bills' due dates? These are very real challenges that will keep us out of our place of peace.

Can we talk about clutter? If you have not used an item in a year, why do you still have it? Is it taking up space for something else that will help you remain focused and in your place of peace? Seek help in these areas. Listen, God cannot get to you what He needs to get to you if you are holding on, fist clenched tight, to the things that are of no value or importance. Clean out that closet. You are blessed to be a blessing to others. There is someone who needs those clothes that you are continuing to hold on to. And those shoes ... Selah.

Check your environment. Is it conducive for your pursuit of peace? I mentioned earlier that people play an important role in your pursuit. Though you will leave some people behind in your pursuit, you will also gain like-minded, purpose-driven people throughout the journey. Be open to hearing from other like-minded individuals. Take advice from those who you desire to emulate. The reason that I checked into a hotel on a Friday afternoon to finish my book is because I took advice from someone who had already written her book. The reason I am drinking water constantly is because I am taking the advice of many who have lost weight and who have encouraged me along my journey.

Not everything and everyone is for you. Recognize *that*. Just as the seasons change, so will your relationships and the activities in which you participate. It is okay to focus on you and your pursuit. What will life look like for you in five years? Pause for a minute. How old (or young) will you be? How long will you have been in your job? Will you have graduated college? Are you still in the same relationship that you have been tolerating? Will you have children, or will you be an empty nester? What needs will you have? I can guarantee you that life will continue to happen. Five years from now will be five years from now. You'll be five years older, *but* will you be in that place of peace or will you still be stuck trying to figure out which direction to move? The time is now to pursue peace. Do not overthink it.

This leads me to another thought about our environment. It is important to address what and who is around us, but we cannot have a successful pursuit without a look at our internal environment. Our mental environment is critical to a meaningful pursuit of peace. We must constantly do a check-up from the neck up. Do you ever think about what you think about? I'll ask it again. Do you ever think about what you are thinking about?

REFLECTION

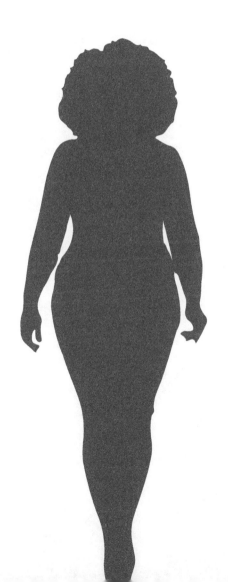

Who are the five people you listen to the most? List them.

_____

_____

_____

_____

_____

_____

_____

_____

_____

_____

_____

_____

_____

_____

_____

_____

_____

_____

_____

Are these people providing you with the assistance needed (directly or indirectly) in your pursuit of peace? If the answer is no, what can you do to find someone else to fill those spots in your top five?

_____

_____

_____

_____

_____

_____

_____

_____

_____

_____

_____

_____

_____

_____

_____

_____

_____

_____

_____

_____

Now, look around. What and who will you need in your space—your environment—to pursue peace, that place where goals are being met and where you are seeing the manifestation of God's promises in your life? What needs to change so that you can begin to prosper? Let me be clear: continue to love people *and* be mindful of the roles they play in your pursuit. It is A-OK to note those who are not directly involved in your pursuit. There will be cheerleaders, and there will be naysayers. Just know the difference and guard your heart and mind accordingly.

Let's examine the *what* that you will need in your pursuit. The *whats* are a necessary part of our environment. When I talk about the *whats*, I am speaking of *things*. What things do you need in order to maintain an environment that is conducive to manifesting your peace? I asked about your thoughts. Where do you keep your thoughts? Are they floating around in your head, or are you writing them down? I suggest writing down your thoughts and dreams. So, the *what* becomes: *what* are you writing your thoughts in? Do you have a journal or notebook that you can keep with you at all times to capture your thoughts and ideas? Maybe you use your smartphone or tablet to capture these thoughts.

Whatever the *what*, identify it. Keep the *what* nearby and have a process to capture your thoughts as they come. Sometimes they come at the most inopportune times, like while you are sleeping. Being awakened out of your sleep to capture your thoughts requires a process. Keep that device or journal (and a pen or pencil) nearby so that you are not searching for them and then talking yourself out of capturing the thought in writing.

Let's talk about your work area, another *what*. What space are you using to meditate, read, write, or otherwise pursue your peace? Oddly, it may be in your bathroom, away from everyone and everything. Now, unless your bathroom is large, well-lit, and somewhat cozy, it may be difficult to stay in there for a long period of time. But where is the place that you go to pull it all together?

I have found that a place that is clutter-free and more organized causes me to focus more on my pursuit. When I have to move things around and find a space to work, think, and write, my focus changes. Decluttering becomes my focus, and I am taking away from the pursuit. Now, if you must first declutter to better define your environment, then, by all means, do so.

Be intentional about creating a space that is yours. What pictures do you have on your walls in that space? Do they push you toward your pursuit, or do they need to change to provide you with more direction and assurance? Whatever you need to create your environment, identify it and then create it.

REFLECTION

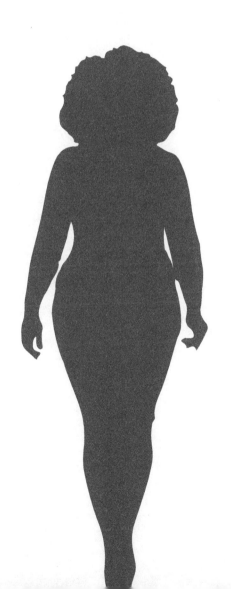

What do you need to do to create an environment conducive to allowing you to enter your place of peace?

_____

_____

_____

_____

_____

_____

_____

_____

_____

_____

_____

_____

_____

_____

_____

_____

_____

_____

_____

What do you need to get rid of? Be honest with yourself. Your peace is on the other side of letting some things go.

_____

_____

_____

_____

_____

_____

_____

_____

_____

_____

_____

_____

_____

_____

_____

_____

_____

_____

_____

_____

What do you need to add to the environment?

_____

_____

_____

_____

_____

_____

_____

_____

_____

_____

_____

_____

_____

_____

_____

_____

_____

_____

_____

_____

_____

ACCOUNTABILITY

We all need an accountability partner in life. This partner may or may not be a friend, but it is someone with whom you can share your goals, dreams, and failures. They must also be someone who will tell it to you straight, no chaser, and who you respect enough to listen to. We often want people in our lives to make us feel good. Your accountability partner is not that person. Your accountability partner will walk with you, push you, and pull you because of their belief in you. Your partner will also tell you when you are not doing your part in the pursuit.

Your accountability partner may not know you need them, so you will have to articulate this. I have found people who possess qualities and skills that I want in my life, and I have watched them. I have asked them to do lunch or dinner just so I can get inside their heads to find out what motivates them. I want to know what they are reading, which podcasts they are listening to, and how they structure their days. And I have asked them to help me.

Yes, we must swallow our pride and know that there are people in this world who will help us along the journey. You may be in a season of life where you are positioned to be an accountability partner to someone else. It goes back to the environment: Who are you surrounded by? If you are the smartest person in your environment, then you need a new environment. Reach out and find someone—or two or three—to whom you can be accountable.

Share with your accountability partner where it is you want to go. This requires that you spend time prioritizing your life. For me, it is God first, family second, and my career or business ventures third. Let me pause here for a second. Putting God first means different things to different people. For me, it centers around relationship, not what we do religiously. My relationship with Christ keeps me focused and grounded. I cast all my cares on Him, knowing that He cares for me. In this, I see God's faithfulness, which develops a trust like none other and a peace that surpasses all understanding. Yes, I attend church, but I am not there every time the church door opens. I say that only because some churches have many different services and fundraising events that require a great deal of time away from your pursuit and your family.

If our relationships with God are not the focus, then the potential for living an unbalanced, religious lifestyle is greatly increased. All successful people have the same amount of time in a day as those who are unsuccessful. What is the difference? Successful people live their lives intentionally, on purpose with a purpose. They have learned to balance their lives.

Second Timothy 1:7 (AMPC) is very clear: "For God did not give us a spirit of timidity (of cowardice, of craven and cringing and fawning fear), but [He has given us a spirit] of power and of love and of calm and well-balanced mind and discipline and self-control." We cannot shy away from successful people. God did not give us a spirit of timidity or fear. We do not need to be intimidated by anyone or anything. Instead, we must operate in the strength of the power that God gives us. He says we can even do things in love, practicing discipline and self-control. That sounds like peace to me.

Let's think about practicing discipline. This is a tough one for me because, until now, I have been guilty of putting other people and other things in front of myself and the goals I desire to achieve. Something I will share that works for me is an affirmation. What are you saying to yourself? What are you thinking about?

REFLECTION

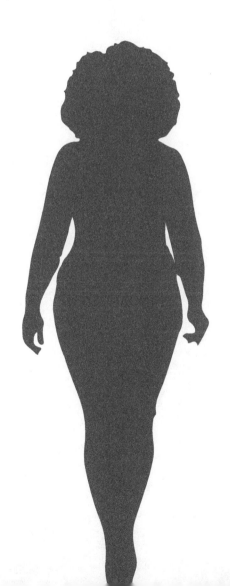

Read these scriptures. What is it that you should be doing in your thought life? What things should you be saying and thinking? Proverbs 18:21 (KJV) says: "Death and life are in the power of the tongue: and they that love it shall eat the fruit thereof."

_____

_____

_____

_____

_____

_____

_____

_____

_____

_____

_____

_____

_____

_____

_____

_____

_____

_____

_____

_____

Philippians 4:8 (NLT): "And now, dear brothers and sisters, one final thing. Fix your thoughts on what is true, and honorable, and right, and pure, and lovely, and admirable. Think about things that are excellent and worthy of praise."

_____

_____

_____

_____

_____

_____

_____

_____

_____

_____

_____

_____

_____

_____

_____

_____

_____

_____

_____

Matthew 21:22 (AMP): "And whatever you ask for in prayer, having faith and [really] believing, you will receive."

_____

_____

_____

_____

_____

_____

_____

_____

_____

_____

_____

_____

_____

_____

_____

_____

_____

_____

_____

Isaiah 55:11 (AMP): "So shall My word be that goes forth out of My mouth: it shall not return to Me void [without producing any effect, useless], but it shall accomplish that which I please *and* purpose, and it shall prosper in the thing for which I sent it."

_____

_____

_____

_____

_____

_____

_____

_____

_____

_____

_____

_____

_____

_____

_____

_____

_____

_____

_____

_____

Mark 11:22–23 (NLT): "Then Jesus said to the disciples, "Have faith in God. I tell you the truth, you can say to this mountain, 'May you be lifted up and thrown into the sea,' and it will happen. But you must really believe it will happen and have no doubt in your heart."

First Peter 3:10–11 (NLT): "For the Scriptures say, "If you want to enjoy life and see many happy days, keep your tongue from speaking evil and your lips from telling lies. Turn away from evil and do good. Search for peace, and work to maintain it.""

Don't just skip through this reflection. Read and meditate on the scriptures. Reflect on what they mean to you and how you will use them to continue your pursuit.

Cast your vision.

The reason you want to think so much about what you are saying is so that you can appropriately cast and create your vision. Your words have creative ability. I'll say it again: Your words have creative ability. You will have whatever things you say. If you know that God has given you a vision of your peaceful state or your successful place, then you want to see that manifest. Do not speak against it or contrary to it. If you desire to lose weight but you say things like, "I'll never lose weight," then you are negating what it is that you believe. Cast your vision confidently. I used to struggle with this. Doubt and fear would set in and I would think, "Suppose I say this and share it with people, and it doesn't manifest. I am going to look silly."

Let me suggest this way of thinking. Suppose you say it and it manifests. We must stop self-sabotaging our lives. We must believe that we will have what we are saying, and we must continue the pursuit until we see it or until God gives us another direction. One thing about God is that He is faithful. Remember that He delights Himself in seeing us do well. He really is a good, good Father, and He wants the best for us.

As you cast your vision, yes, there will be some who say you cannot obtain it. They may say nothing in support of you, or they may say things that diminish your vision and dim your light. No worries. That is to be expected. Remember, it is *your* vision, not their vision.

I love it when people show me who they are by opening their mouths. I no longer have to figure out whether they are for me. I thank God that I see their true colors, and I keep moving in the direction of my peace. Do not get caught up in what *they* say. Keep saying what God has said and watch your peace, which surpasses all understanding, manifest.

Where do you see yourself?

REFLECTION

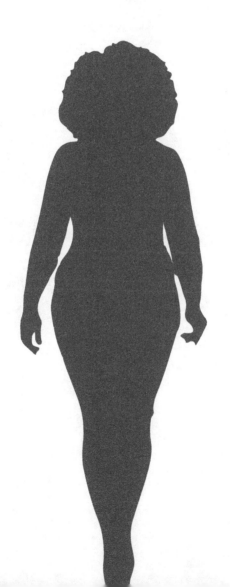

Have you written the vision for your life? How will you know when you have entered that place of peace? What will it look like?

_____

_____

_____

_____

_____

_____

_____

_____

_____

_____

_____

_____

_____

_____

_____

_____

_____

_____

_____

_____

Habakkuk 2:3 (MSG) gives us directions that are powerful. "And then God answered: 'Write this. Write what you see. Write it out in big block letters so that it can be read on the run. This vision-message is a witness pointing to what's coming. It aches for the coming—it can hardly wait!"

As you write the vision (and I encourage you to do it now; there is no need to wait until the first of the year or the first of the month or the first of the week. Today is your day one.), get excited! With God's help and your willingness to pursue your peace, your vision will come to pass. Get excited about the journey and what you will learn along the way. Get excited about who you will meet on the journey!

Get excited about your personal growth and development and find ...

ENJOYMENT

Aaaaah … enjoyment! (Insert smile here.) As a matter of fact, smile often. Smile big, radiant smiles. Whether you have two, thirty-two, or somewhere in between, show your teeth. Check to see if you have dimples. Keep smiling. Smile because you can open your eyes. Smile because you can read this, or smile because you can hear someone reading it to you.

Did you have anything to eat today? Smile because of that. Did you wear any type of clothing? Smile. Smile because you have one friend, and smile bigger if you can think of one person, just one, who thinks enough of you to dislike you. Yep, that too, is a reason to smile. Do you have pain in your body? You can feel it? Smile for that. If you can smile and you don't, shame on you.

REFLECTION

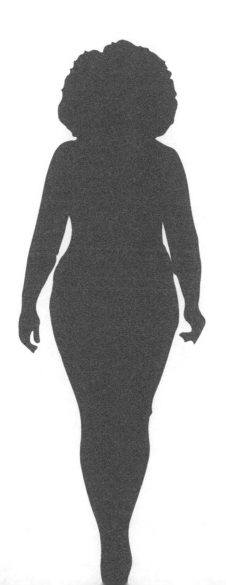

What other things or people bring enjoyment to your life? What can you smile about?

_____

_____

_____

_____

_____

_____

_____

_____

_____

_____

_____

_____

_____

_____

_____

_____

_____

_____

_____

_____

If you're thinking, "I don't have a reason to smile. My life is completely upside down," smile anyway. If you can imagine a way out, you can get out of that situation to a place where you can enjoy life.

Life is precious. Enjoy it! Where is that place of enjoyment for you? Does it involve others, or is it a place you go to be all alone? Is it in a mountainous location where all you can see are hills and trails, or is your place one of solace where you watch a river flow and fish swim calmly in their natural habitat? Wherever you place is, get there. Get there physically, get there mentally, get there virtually—but get there.

Just to share a snippet of how I *know* you can find the missing *peace* to life's puzzle, I have overcome a huge work-related situation where racist acts, hatred, and jealousy almost caused me to lose not just my job, but my career.

I was a caretaker for my mother at the time, whose health was declining due to her battle with uterine cancer. At the same time, I was blessed to become a mother to a teenage mother, which makes me a loving grandmother (insert smile). That teenage mother is now a college student and an entrepreneur who works to take care of her amazing son. (She will tell her story in another book—and quite the story it is.) I am the only sister to my older brother who, during the same time, was facing a medical challenge. You know that medical challenge that starts with a *C*? Yeah, you guessed it, prostate cancer. And did I include that I was still grieving the death of my father, who had taken his last breath only a year before my mother was diagnosed with cancer?

ENJOYMENT

What of those things could I have controlled? Very few, if any. I know firsthand how difficult life can be. I share that only because it is easy to tell someone how things should be when you've never experienced anything. I know the pursuit is not always easy. It was not easy for me, but it was and continues to be necessary.

Life happens fast. Enjoy it.

My happy place is quietly sitting at the beach. I don't people watch; neither do I care about the heat or the cold chill. You see, I can go to the beach at any time of the year. My body type is my body type, and I am not consumed with wearing a bikini or even a swimsuit. I can sit in a lightweight, free-flowing dress and be content. At the beach, it's not about anything other than "being" at the beach. I give myself permission to be present at the beach, taking in all of God's handiwork—sitting, listening to the seagulls, closing my eyes, and basking in the sunlight while listening to the waves crash against each other. The laughter, or even the blessed quietness—all of it, I love and embrace.

Music is another tool that I use to showcase my enjoyment of life. Yes, as a believer, I listen to all types of music. The beat is usually the first attraction for me, but the lyrics will be the keeper. Music allows me to express my feelings and, at times, causes me to drift away to explore possibilities. With lyrics like "I believe I can fly. I believe I can touch the sky" or Tamela Mann's rendition of "I Can Only Imagine," I'm there, tears flowing, thinking about what it will be like to see Jesus. I can only imagine. After closing my mouth from being in awe of those moments, I am motivated to live my best life so that I can live again.

Although I am not the best dancer, I love to *move*! (*Move* is the gentler, kinder, more acceptable word that I use in place of the word *exercise*.) Even in my most obese state, I can find enjoyment in breaking a sweat from movement. I can chuckle on my beaten path, back and forth to the bathroom, from consuming my gallon of water each day, one ounce at a time.

Life is full of enjoyment.

You will find the missing peace to life's puzzle. I believe in you. You've got this!

Isaiah 26:3 promises that if you keep your mind stayed on Him, He will keep you in perfect peace.

PEACE

Pursuit

Environment

Accountability

Casting

Enjoyment

SCRIPTURES TO ASSIST AS YOU FIND PEACE

"Many are the afflictions of the righteous: but the LORD has delivered him out of them all" (Psalm 34:19 KJV).

"The thief comes not but for to steal, and to kill, and to destroy: I am come that they may have life, and that they might have it more abundantly" (John 10:10 KJV).

"Blessed are the peacemakers: for they shall be called the children of God. Blessed are they which are persecuted for righteousness' sake: for theirs is the kingdom of heaven" (Matthew 5:9–10 KJV).

"For I know the thoughts that I think toward you, saith the Lord, thoughts of peace, and not of evil, to give you an expected end" (Jeremiah 29:11 KJV).

"Beloved, I wish above all things that you may prosper and be in health, even as your soul prospers" (3 John 1:2 NKJV).

"No good thing will God withhold from you as you walk uprightly before Him" (Psalm 84:11b KJV).

"Cast not away therefore your confidence, which hath great recompence of reward" (Hebrews 11:35 KJV).

"He that dwells in the secret place of the most High shall abide under the shadow of the Almighty" (Psalm 91:1 KJV).

"The Lord is my light and my salvation; whom shall I fear? The Lord is the strength of my life: of whom shall I be afraid?" (Psalm 27:1 KJV).

"I had fainted, unless I had believed to see the goodness of the Lord in the land of the living. Wait on the Lord: be of good courage, and he shall strengthen thine heart; wait, I say, on the Lord" (Psalm 27:13–14KJV).

"My brethren, count it all joy when ye fall into divers temptations; Knowing this, that the trying of your faith worketh patience. But let patience have her perfect work, that ye may be perfect and entire, wanting nothing. If any of you lack wisdom, let him ask of God, that giveth to all men liberally, and upbraideth not; and it shall be given him. But let him ask in faith, nothing wavering. For he that wavereth is like a wave of the sea driven with the wind and tossed. For let no that man think that he shall receive any thing of the Lord." (James 1:2–7 KJV)

"Peace I leave with you, my peace I give unto you; not as the world giveth, give I unto you. Let not your heart be troubled, neither let it be afraid" (John 14:27 KJV).

"Be careful for nothing; but in everything by prayer and supplication with thanksgiving let your requests be made known unto God. And the peace of God, which passeth all understanding, shall keep your hearts and minds through Christ Jesus" (Philippians 4:6–7 KJV).

"Finally, brethren, whatsoever things are true, whatsoever things are honest, whatsoever things are just, whatsoever things are pure, whatsoever things are lovely, whatsoever thing are of good report; if there be any virtue, and if there be any praise, think on these things. These things, which ye have both learned, and received, and heard, and seen in me, do: and the God of peace shall be with you" (Philippians 4:8–9 KJV).

"If it be possible, as much as lieth in you, live peaceably with all men. Dearly beloved, avenge not yourselves, but rather give place unto wrath; for it is written, Vengeance is mine: I will repay, saith the Lord" (Romans 12:18–19 KJV).

"It is of the Lord's mercies that we are not consumed, because his compassions fail not. They are new every morning; great is thy faithfulness" (Lamentations 3:22–23 KJV).

MY PRAYER

Dear God,

Thank you for allowing me to write this book. I pray that everyone who reads it receives something valuable that will help them truly find the missing *peace* in their lives.

In Jesus's name.

Amen.

ABOUT THE AUTHOR

Ethel E. Reeves wears a smile as a testament of God's love and faithfulness, knowing that she is fearfully and wonderfully made. As a native of Lynchburg, Virginia, she is distinguished in many realms: she is a mother, a grandmother, a cosmetologist, an entrepreneur, and a passionate educator and encourager. As the founder of The Encouragement Group, Ethel believes in providing people with the skills and confidence necessary to maximize the greatness that exists inside them. She is a powerfully engaging speaker who has facilitated workshops and addressed audiences for various organizations and ministries. Her genuine spirit allows her to meet people where they are and to uplift them.

For more information about scheduling Ethel E. Reeves, passionate educator and encourager, visit www.ethelreeves.com

CPSIA information can be obtained
at www.ICGtesting.com
Printed in the USA
BVHW030157300821
615542BV00020B/128